Books by Anthony Hecht

THE VENETIAN VESPERS (1979)

MILLIONS OF STRANGE SHADOWS (1977)

THE HARD HOURS (1967)

A SUMMONING OF STONES (1954)

Translation

AESCHYLUS' SEVEN AGAINST THEBES (1973)
(with Helen Bacon)

THE
VENETIAN
VESPERS

THE VENETIAN VESPERS

POEMS BY

ANTHONY HECHT

Atheneum   New York   *1980*

The following poems were originally published as follows:

THE GRAPES: *The American Scholar*
THE DEODAND: *Kenyon Review*
INVECTIVE AGAINST DENISE, A WITCH: *The American Scholar*
AUSPICES: *The New Republic*
APPLICATION FOR A GRANT: *Times Literary Supplement*
AN OVERVIEW: *Marxist Perspectives*
STILL LIFE: *Antaeus*
PERSISTENCES: *Ploughshares*
A CAST OF LIGHT: *The New Leader*
THE VENETIAN VESPERS: *Poetry*

The versions of the two poems of Joseph Brodsky were made for his book of poems, *A Part of Speech*, published by Farrar, Strauss, Giroux, 1979, copyright © 1979 by Farrar, Straus & Giroux, Inc.

THE VENETIAN VESPERS appeared first in book form in a limited edition published by David R. Godine, copyright © 1979 by Anthony E. Hecht.

For HELEN

Whatever pain is figured in these pages,
　　　Whatever voice here grieves,
Belonged to other lives and distant ages
　　　Mnemosyne retrieves;
But all the joys and forces of invention
　　　That can transmute to true
Gold these base matters floated in suspension
　　　Are due alone to you.

Thou must be patient. We came crying hither;
Thou know'st, the first time that we smell the air
We wawl and cry.

King Lear, IV, vi, 182–4

Though in many of its aspects this visible world seems
formed in love, the invisible spheres were formed in fright.

Moby Dick, CH. XLII

Muss es sein?
Es muss sein!
Es muss sein!
BEETHOVEN, *Quartet #16 in F major,*
opus 135

CONTENTS

I

THE GRAPES

At five o'clock of a summer afternoon
We are already shadowed by the mountain
On whose lower slopes we perch, all of us here
At the *Hôtel de l'Univers et Déjeuner.*
The fruit trees and the stone lions out front
In deepening purple silhouette themselves
Against the bright green fields across the valley
Where, at the *Beau Rivage*, patrons are laved
In generous tides of gold. At cocktail time
Their glasses glint like gems, while we're eclipsed.
Which may explain
Why the younger set, which likes to get up late,
Assess its members over aperitifs,
Prefers that western slope, while we attract
A somewhat older, quieter clientele,
Americans mostly, though they seem to come
From everywhere, and are usually good tippers.
Still, it is strange and sad, at cocktail time,
To look across the valley from our shade,
As if from premature death, at all that brilliance
Across which silently on certain days
Shadows of clouds slide past in smooth parade,
While even our daisies and white irises
Are filled with blues and darkened premonitions.
Yet for our patrons, who are on holiday,
Questions of time are largely set aside.
They are indulgently amused to find
All the news magazines on the wicker table
In the lobby are outrageously outdated.
But Madame likes to keep them on display;
They add a touch of color, and a note
Of home and habit for many, and it's surprising
How thoroughly they are read on rainy days.
And I myself have smuggled one or two
Up to my bedroom, there to browse upon
Arrested time in *Time, Incorporated.*

3

The Grapes

There it is always 1954,
And Marlon Brando, perfectly preserved,
Sullen and brutal and desirable,
Avoids my eyes with a scowl; the record mile
Always belongs to Roger Bannister;
The rich and sleek of the international set
Are robbed of their furs and diamonds, get divorced
In a world so far removed from the rest of us
It almost seems arranged for our amusement
As they pose for pictures, perfectly made-up,
Coiffeured by Mr. Charles, languid, serene.
They never show up here—our little resort
Is far too mean for them—except in my daydreams.
My dreams at night are reserved for Marc-Antoine,
One of the bellboys at the *Beau Rivage*.
In his striped vest with flat buttons of brass
He comes to me every night after my prayers,
In fantasy, of course; in actual fact
He's taken no notice of me whatsoever.
Quite understandable, for I must be
Easily ten years older than he, and only
A chambermaid. As with all the very young,
To him the future's limitless and bright,
Anything's possible, one has but to wait.
No doubt it explains his native cheerfulness.
No doubt he dreams of a young millionairess,
Beautiful, spoiled and ardent, at his feet.
Perhaps it shall come to pass. Such things have happened.
Even barmaids and pantry girls have been seen
Translated into starlets tanning themselves
At the end of a diving board. But just this morning
Something came over me like the discovery
Of a deep secret of the universe.
It was early. I was in the dining room
Long before breakfast was served. I was alone.
Mornings, of course, it's we who get the light,
An especially tender light, hopeful and soft.

I stood beside a table near a window,
Gazing down at a crystal bowl of grapes
In ice-water. They were green grapes, or, rather,
They were a sort of pure, unblemished jade,
Like turbulent ocean water, with misted skins,
Their own pale, smoky sweat, or tiny frost.
I leaned over the table, letting the sun
Fall on my forearm, contemplating them.
Reflections of the water dodged and swam
In nervous incandescent filaments
Over my blouse and up along the ceiling.
And all those little bags of glassiness,
Those clustered planets, leaned their eastern cheeks
Into the sunlight, each one showing a soft
Meridian swelling where the thinning light
Mysteriously tapered into shadow,
To cool recesses, to the tranquil blues
That then were pillowing the *Beau Rivage*.
And watching I could almost see the light
Edge slowly over their simple surfaces,
And feel the sunlight moving on my skin
Like a warm glacier. And I seemed to know
In my blood the meaning of sidereal time
And know my little life had somehow crested.
There was nothing left for me now, nothing but years.
My destiny was cast and Marc-Antoine
Would not be called to play a part in it.
His passion, his Dark Queen, he'd meet elsewhere.
And I knew at last, with a faint, visceral twitch,
A flood of weakness that comes to the resigned,
What it must have felt like in that rubber boat
In mid-Pacific, to be the sole survivor
Of a crash, idly dandled on that blank
Untroubled waste, and see the light decline,
Taper and fade in graduated shades
Behind the International Date Line—
An accident I read about in *Time*.

THE DEODAND

What are these women up to? They've gone and strung
Drapes over the windows, cutting out light
And the slightest hope of a breeze here in mid-August.
Can this be simply to avoid being seen
By some prying *femme-de-chambre* across the boulevard
Who has stepped out on a balcony to disburse
Her dustmop gleanings on the summer air?
And what of these rugs and pillows, all haphazard,
Here in what might be someone's living room
In the swank, high-toned sixteenth *arrondissement?*
What would their fathers, husbands, *fiancés,*
Those pillars of the old *haute-bourgeoisie,*
Think of the strange charade now in the making?
Swathed in exotic finery, in loose silks,
Gauzy organzas with metallic threads,
Intricate Arab vests, brass ornaments
At wrist and ankle, those small sexual fetters,
Tight little silver chains, and bangled gold
Suspended like a coarse barbarian treasure
From soft earlobes pierced through symbolically,
They are preparing some *tableau vivant.*
One girl, consulting the authority
Of a painting, perhaps by Ingres or Delacroix,
Is reporting over her shoulder on the use
Of kohl to lend its dark, savage allurements.
Another, playing the slave-artisan's role,
Almost completely naked, brush in hand,
Attends to these instructions as she prepares
To complete the seductive shadowing of the eyes
Of the blonde girl who appears the harem favorite,
And who is now admiring these effects
In a mirror held by a fourth, a well-clad servant.
The scene simmers with Paris and women in heat,
Darkened and airless, perhaps with a faint hum
Of trapped flies, and a strong odor of musk.
For whom do they play at this hot indolence

And languorous vassalage? They are alone
With fantasies of jasmine and brass lamps,
Melons and dates and bowls of rose-water,
A courtyard fountain's firework blaze of prisms,
Its basin sown with stars and *poissons d'or*,
And a rude stable smell of animal strength,
Of leather thongs, hinting of violations,
Swooning lubricities and lassitudes.
What is all this but crude imperial pride,
Feminized, scented and attenuated,
The exploitation of the primitive,
Homages of romantic self-deception,
Mimes of submission glamorized as lust?
Have they no intimation, no recall
Of the once queen who liked to play at milkmaid,
And the fierce butcher-reckoning that followed
Her innocent, unthinking masquerade?
Those who will not be taught by history
Have as their curse the office to repeat it,
And for this little spiritual debauch
(Reported here with warm, exacting care
By Pierre Renoir in 1872—
Apparently unnoticed by the girls,
An invisible voyeur, like you and me)
Exactions shall be made, an expiation,
A forfeiture. Though it take ninety years,
All the retributive iron of Racine
Shall answer from the raging heat of the desert.

    In the final months of the Algerian war
They captured a very young French Legionnaire.
They shaved his head, decked him in a blonde wig,
Carmined his lips grotesquely, fitted him out
With long, theatrical false eyelashes
And a bright, loose-fitting skirt of calico,
And cut off all the fingers of both hands.
He had to eat from a fork held by his captors.

Thus costumed, he was taken from town to town,
Encampment to encampment, on a leash,
And forced to beg for his food with a special verse
Sung to a popular show tune of those days:
"Donnez moi à manger de vos mains
Car c'est pour vous que je fais ma petite danse;
Car je suis Madeleine, la putain,
Et je m'en vais le lendemain matin,
Car je suis La Belle France."

THE SHORT END

Here the anthem doth commence:
Love and Constancy is dead,
Phoenix and the turtle fled
In a mutual flame from hence.

I

"Greetings from Tijuana!" on a ground
Of ripe banana rayon with a fat
And couchant Mexican in mid-siesta,
Wrapped in a many-colored Jacobin
Serape, and more deeply rapt in sleep,
Head propped against a phallic organ cactus
Of shamrock green, all thrown against a throw
Of purple on a Biedermeier couch—
This is the latest prize, newly unwrapped,
A bright and shiny capstone to the largest
Assemblage of such pillows in the East:
Pillows from Kennebunkport, balsam-scented
And stuffed with woodchips, pillows from Coney Island
Blazoned with Ferris Wheels and Roller Coasters,
Pillows that fart when sat on, tasselled pillows
From Old New Orleans, creole and redly carnal,
And what may be the gem of the collection,
From the New York World's Fair of Thirty-Nine,
Bearing a white Trylon and Perisphere,
Moderne, severe and thrilling, on the recto;
And on the verso in gold and blue italics
The Fair's motto: "A Century of Progress."
To this exciting find, picked up for pennies
At a garage sale in Schenectady
(Though slightly soiled with ketchup at one corner)
Yosemite, Niagara, Honolulu
Have yielded place, meekly accepting exile
In the mud room, the conversation pit,
Or other unpeopled but bepillowed rooms.

This far-flung empire, these domains belong
To Shirley Carson and her husband, "Kit,"
Softening the hard edges of their lives.
Shirley is curator, museum guide,
The Mellon and the Berenson of these
Mute instances (except for the hidden farts)
Of fustian and of bombast, crocheted, embroidered
And stencilled with bright Day-Glo coloring.
They cheer her with their brilliance, with their sleek
And traveled worldliness, and serve as cover,
In the literal sense, a plumped and bolstered cover,
For the booze she needs to have always at hand.
There used to be a game, long since abandoned,
In which he'd try to find what she concealed.
"Cooler," she'd say, "yer gettin' really icy,"
She'd say, "so whyantcha fix yerself a drink?"
As he sought vainly behind Acapulco,
All flame and orange satin, or underneath
A petit point of moviedom's nobility :
A famous, genuine Hollywood Marquee,
Below which stood a spurious Romanov.
He quit because she always had reserves,
What she called "liquid assets," tucked away.
He had tried everything over the years.
There was no appealing to her vanity;
She was now puffily fat and pillowy.
Reason, of course, was futile, and he'd learned
That strong-arm methods strengthened her defiance.
These days he came home from the body shop
He owned and operated, its walls thumb-tacked
With centerfolded bodies from *Playboy*,
Yielding, expectant, invitational,
Came home oil-stained and late to find her drunk
And the house rank with the staleness of dead butts.
Staleness, that's what it was, he used to say
To himself, trying to figure what went wrong,
Emptying ashtrays of their ghostly wreckage,

Their powders and cremations of the past.
He always went to bed long before she did.
She would sit up till late, smoking and drinking,
Afloat upon a wild surfeit of colors,
The midway braveries, harlequin streamers,
Or skewbald, carney liveries of the macaw,
Through which, from time to time, memories arose.

II

    Of these, two were persistent. In one of them
She was back in the first, untainted months of marriage,
Slight, shy, and dressed in soft ecru charmeuse,
Hopeful, adoring, and in return adored
By her husband, who was then a traveling salesman.
The company had scheduled a convention
In Atlantic City, and had generously
Invited the men to bring along their wives.
They were to stay in triumph at the Marlborough-
Blenheim, a luxury resort hotel
That ran both fresh and salt water in its tubs,
And boasted an international string ensemble
That assembled every afternoon at four
For *thé dansant*, when the very air was rich
With Jerome Kern, Romberg, and Rudolph Friml.
The room they were assigned gave on an air shaft
But even so they could smell the black Atlantic,
And being hidden away, she told herself,
Was just the thing for newlyweds, and made
Forays on the interminable vista
Of the boardwalk—it seemed to stretch away
In hazy diminution, like the prospects
Or boxwood avenues of a chateau—
The more exciting. Or so it seemed in prospect.
She recalled the opulent soft wind-chime music,

A mingling of silverware and ice-water
At their first breakfast in the dining room.
Also another sound. That of men's voices
Just slightly louder than was necessary
For the table-mates they seemed to be addressing.
It bore some message, all that baritone
Brio of masculine snort and self-assertion.
It belonged with cigars and bets and locker rooms.
It had nothing to do with damask and chandeliers.
It was a sign, she knew at once, of something.
They wore her husband's same convention badge,
So must be salesmen, here for a pep talk
And booster from top-level management,
Young, hopeful, energetic, just like him,
But, in some way she found unnerving, louder.
That was the earliest omen.
                            The second was
The vast boardwalk itself, its herringbone
Of seasoned lumber lined on the inland side
By Frozen Custard booths, Salt Water Taffy
Kneaded and stretched by large industrial cams,
Pinball and shooting galleries with Kewpie Dolls,
Pink dachshunds, cross-eyed ostriches for prizes,
Fun Houses, Bumpum Cars and bowling alleys,
And shops that offered the discriminating
Hand-decorated shells, fantastic landscapes
Entirely composed of varnished star-fish,
And other shops displaying what was called
"Sophisticated Nightwear For My Lady,"
With black-lace panties bearing a crimson heart
At what might be Mons Veneris' timber-line,
Flesh-toned brassieres with large rose-window cutouts
Edged with elaborate guimpe, rococo portholes
Allowing the nipples to assert themselves,
And see-through nightgowns bordered with angora
Or frowsy feather boas of magenta.
Here she was free to take the healthful airs,

Inhale the unclippered trade-winds of New Jersey
And otherwise romp and disport herself
From nine until five-thirty, when her husband,
Her only Norman, would be returned to her.
Such was this place, a hapless rural seat
And sandy edge of the Truck Garden State,
The dubious North American Paradise.

III

It was just after dinner their second evening
That a fellow-conventioneer, met in the lobby,
Invited them to join a little party
For a libation in the Plantagenet Bar
And Tap Room; he performed the introductions
To Madge and Felix, Bubbles and Billy Jim,
Astrid, and lastly, to himself, Maurice,
Whose nickname, it appeared, was Two Potato,
And things were on a genial, first-name basis
Right from the start, so it was only after
The second round of drinks (which both the Carsons
Intended as their last, and a sufficient
Fling at impromptu sociability)
That it was inadvertently discovered
That the Carsons were little more than newlyweds
On what amounted to their honeymoon.
No one would hear of them leaving, or trying to pay
For anything. Another round of drinks
Was ordered. Two Potato proclaimed himself
Their host, and winked at them emphatically.
There followed much raucous, suggestive toasting,
Norman was designated "a stripling kid,"
And ceremoniously nicknamed "Kit,"
And people started calling Shirley "Shirl,"
And "Curly-Shirl" and "Shirl-Girl." There were displays

13

Of mock-tenderness towards the young couple
And gags about the missionary position,
With weak, off-key, off-color, attempts at singing
"Rock of Ages," with hands clasped in prayer
And eyes raised ceilingward at "cleft for me,"
Eyes closed at "let me hide myself in thee,"
The whole number grotesquely harmonized
In the manner of a barbershop quartet.
By now she wanted desperately to leave
But couldn't figure out the way to do so
Without giving offense, seeming ungrateful;
And somehow, she suspected, they knew this.
Two Potato particularly seemed
Aggressive both in his solicitude
And in the smirking lewdness of his jokes
As he unblushingly eyed the bride for blushes
And gallantly declared her "a good sport,"
"A regular fella," and "the little woman."
She knew when the next round of drinks appeared
That she and Norman were mere hostages
Whom nobody would ransom. Billy Jim asked
If either of them knew a folk-song called
"The Old Gism Trail," and everybody laughed,
Laughed at the plain vulgarity itself
And at the Carsons' manifest discomfort
And at their pained, inept attempt at laughter.
The merriment was acid and complex.
Felix it was who kept proposing toasts
To "good ol' Shirl an' Kit," names which he slurred
Both in pronunciation and disparagement
With an expansive, wanton drunkenness
That in its license seemed soberly planned
To increase by graduated steps until
Without seeming aware of what he was doing
He'd raise a toast to "good ol' Curl an' Shit."
They managed to get away before that happened,
Though Shirley knew in her bones it was intended,

Had seen it coming from a mile away.
They left, but not before it was made clear
That they were the only married couple present,
That the other men had left their wives at home,
And that this was what conventions were all about.
The Carsons were made to feel laughably foolish,
Timid and prepubescent and repressed,
And with a final flourish of raised glasses
The "guests" were at last permitted to withdraw.

IV

Fade-out; assisted by a dram of gin,
And a soft radio soundtrack bringing up
A velvety chanteur who wants a kiss
By wire, in some access of chastity,
Yet in a throaty passion volunteers,
"Baby, mah heart's on fire." Fade-in with pan
Shot of a highway somewhere south of Wheeling
Where she and her husband, whom she now calls Kit,
Were driving through a late day in November
Toward some goal obscure as the very weather,
Defunctive, moist, overcast, requiescent.
Rounding a bend, they came in sudden view
Of what seemed a caravan of trucks and cars,
A long civilian convoy, parked along
The right-hand shoulder, and instantly slowed down,
Fearing a speed-trap or an accident.
It was instead, as a billboard announced,
A LIVE ENTOMBMENT—CONTRIBUTIONS PLEASE.
They found a parking slot, directed by
Two courteous State Troopers with leather holsters
That seemed tumescent with heavy, flopping side-arms,
And made their way across the stony ground
To a strange, silent crowd, as at a grave-side.

A poster fixed to a tree gave the details :
"Here lies George Rose in a casket supplied by
The Memento Morey Funeral Home of Wheeling.
He has been underground 38 days.
[The place for the numbers was plastered with new stickers.]
He lives on liquids and almond Hershey bars
Fed through the speaking tube next to his head,
By which his brother and custodian,
John Wesley Rose, communicates with him,
And by means of which he breathes. Note that the tube
Can be bent sideways to keep out the rain.
Visitors are invited to put all questions
To the custodian because George Rose
Is eager to preserve his solitude.
He has forsworn the vanities of this world.
Donations will be gratefully accepted."
At length she wedged her way among the curious
To where she saw a varnished pine-wood box
With neatly mitred corners, fitted with glass
At the top, and measuring roughly a foot square,
Sunk in the earth, protruding about three inches.
Through this plain aperture she now beheld
The pale, expressionless features of George Rose,
Bearded, but with a pocked, pitted complexion,
And pale blue eyes conveying by their blankness
A boredom so profound it might indeed
Pass for a certain otherworldliness,
Making it eminently clear to all
That not a single face that showed itself
Against the sky for his consideration
Was found by him to be beautiful or wise
Or worthy of the least notice or interest.
One could tell he was alive because he blinked.
At the crowd's edge, near the collection box,
Stood a man who was almost certainly his brother,
Caretaker and custodian, engaged
In earnest talk with one of the State Troopers.

It crossed her mind to wonder how they dealt
With his evacuations, yet she couldn't
Ask such a question of an unknown man.
But Kit seemed to have questions of his own
And as he approached John Wesley she turned away
To the edge of a large field and stood alone
In some strange wordless seizure of distress.
She turned her gaze deliberately away
From the road, the cars, the little clustered knot
Of humankind around that sheet of glass,
Like flies around a dish of sweetened water,
And focused intently on what lay before her.
A grizzled landscape, burdock and thistle-choked,
A snarled, barbed-wire barricade of brambles,
All thorn and needle-sharp hostility.
The dead weeds wicker-brittle, raffia-pale,
The curled oak leaves a deep tobacco brown,
The sad rouge of old bricks, chips of cement
From broken masonry, a stubble field
Like a mangy lion's pelt of withered grass.
Off in the distance a thoroughly dead tree,
Peeled of its bark, sapless, an armature
Of well-groomed, military, silver-gray.
And other leafless trees, their smallest twigs
Incising a sky the color of a bruise.
In all the rancid, tannic, mustard tones,
Mud colors, lignum grays and mottled rocks,
The only visible relief she found
Was the plush red velvet of the sumac spikes
And the slick, vinyl, Stygian, anthracite
Blackness of water in a drainage ditch.
The air sang with the cold of empty caves,
Of mildew, cobwebs, slug and maggot life.
And at her feet, among the scattered stubs
Of water-logged non-filter cigarettes,
Lay a limp length of trampled fennel stalk.
And then she heard, astonishingly close,

17

Right at her side, the incontestable voice
Of someone who could not possibly be there :
Of old Miss McIntosh, her eleventh grade
Latin instructor, now many years dead,
Saying with slow, measured authority,
"It is your duty to remain right here.
Those people and their cars will go away.
Norman will go. George Rose will stay where he is,
But you have nothing whatever to do with him.
He will die quietly inside his coffin.
From time to time you will be given water
And a peanut butter sandwich on white bread.
You will stay here as long as it shall take
To love this place so much you elect to stay
Forever, forsaking all others you have known
Or dreamed of or incontinently longed for.
Look at and meditate upon the crows.
Think upon God. Humbly prepare yourself,
Like the wise virgins in the parable,
For the coming resurrection of George Rose.
Consider deeply why as the first example
Of the first conjugation—which is not
As conjugal as some suppose—one learns
The model verb forms of 'to love,' *amare*,
Which also happens to be the word for 'bitter.'
Both love and Latin are more difficult
Than is usually imagined or admitted.
This is your final exam; this is your classroom."

V

    Another voice drowns out Miss McIntosh.
It's Mel Tormé, singing *Who's Sorry Now?*
Followed by a Kid Ory version of

Quincy Street Stomp, and bringing back in view
The bright upholstery of the present tense,
The lax geography of pillows, gin-
And-bitters with anesthetic bitterness.
It must be three AM, but never mind.
Open upon her lap lies *The New Yorker*,
Exhibiting a full-page color ad
For the Scotch whiskey-based liqueur, Drambuie,
Soft-focus, in the palest tints of dawn.
Therein a lady and a gentleman
Stand gazing north from the triumphal arch
That Stanford White designed for Washington Square.
She wears an evening gown of shocking pink
And a mink stole. Her escort, in black tie,
Standing behind her, his arms about her waist,
Follows her gaze uptown where a peach haze
Is about to infuse the windows of the rich.
Meanwhile, this couple, who have just descended
From a hansom cab departing towards the east,
Have all Fifth Avenue stretched out before them
In Élysée prospectus, like the calm fields
Where Attic heroes dwell. They are alone
On the blank street. The truths of economics,
The dismal (decimal) science, dissolve away
In the faint light, and leave her standing there,
Shirley herself, suddenly slim again,
In the arms of a young nameless gentleman.
To be sure, the salmon hues up in the eighties,
Flushing the Metropolitan's facade,
Glinting on silver tops of skyscrapers
As upon factory-made, hand-polished Alps
(Though the deep canyons still repose in darkness)
Bespeak the calm beneficence of dawn
When they shall both raise up their brandy glasses
Filled with that admirable Scotch liqueur
Or else with gin and tolerable bitters

And toast each other in some nearby penthouse.
But meanwhile her attention is wholly drawn
To the carriage lantern on the hansom cab.
A kerosene lantern with a concave shield
Or chrome reflector inside a box of glass.
The quivering flame of the broad ribbon wick
Itself presents a quick array of colors,
All brilliance, light, intensity and hope.
The flames flow upward from a rounded base
Like an inverted waterfall of gold,
Yet somehow at the center, the pure kernel
Of fire is pearly, incandescent white.
Out of that whiteness all the celestial hues
Of dawn proliferate in wobbly spectra,
Lilac and orange, the rust of marigold,
The warm and tropic colors of the world
That she inhabits, that she has collected
And stuffed like assorted trophies of the kill.
The shape of flames is almond-like, the shape
Of Egyptian eyes turned sideways, garlic cloves,
Camel-hair tips of watercolor brushes,
Of waterdrops. The shape performs a dance,
A sinuous, erotic wavering,
All inference and instability,
Shimmy and glitter. It is, she suddenly knows,
The figure *redivivus* of George Rose,
Arisen, youthful, strong and roseate,
Tiny, of course, pathetically reduced
To pinky size, but performing a lewd dance
Of Shiva, the rippling muscles of his thighs
And abdomen as fluent as a river
Of upward-pouring color, the golden finish
Of Sardanapalus, emphatic rhythms
Of blues and body language, a centrifuge
Of climbing braids that beautifully enlarge,
Thicken and hang pendulous in the air.
Out of these twinings, foldings, envelopings

Of brass and apricot, biceps and groin,
She sees the last thing she will ever see :
The purest red there is, passional red,
Fire-engine red, the red of Valentines,
Of which she is herself the howling center.

INVECTIVE AGAINST DENISE, A WITCH

The hatred I reserve for thee
Surpasses the malignity
    Of camel and of bear,
Old witch, unseemly thaumaturge,
Whipped by the Public Hangman's scourge
    The length of the town square.

Luring about you, like a brood,
The vulgar, curious and lewd,
    You shamelessly lay bare
Your haunches to the sight of men,
Your naked shoulder, abdomen
    Emblazoned with blood-smear.

And yet that punishment is slight
Compared to what is yours by right;
    Just Heaven must not bestow
Its mercy on so foul a thing
But rather by its whirlwind bring
    Such proud excesses low.

Still wracked by the brute overthrow
The Titans suffered long ago,
    A brooding Mother Earth,
To spite the Gods, in her old age
Shall, in an ecstasy of rage,
    At last bring you to birth.

You know the worth and power of both
Rare herbals and concocted broth
    Brought from the tropic zone;
You know the very month and hour
To pluck the lust-inducing flower
    That makes a woman groan.

There's not, among the envenomed plants
On mountain or in valley haunts,
  One that your eyes have missed
And has not yielded up its ground
To your bright sickle-blade, and crowned
  Your formidable quest.

When, like a lunatic, all bare,
The moon lets down its mystic hair
  Of cold, enraging light,
You wrap your features in the hide
Of animals, and smoothly glide
  Abroad into the night.

Your least breath ravishes the blood
Of all dogs in the neighborhood
  And sets them on to bark,
Makes rivers flow uphill, reversed,
And baying wolves observe your cursed
  Hegira through the dark.

Chatelaine of deserted spots,
Of mouldered cemetery plots
  Where you are most at home,
Muttering diabolic runes,
You disinter the troubled bones
  From their sequestered tomb.

To grieve a mother more you don
The aspect of her only son
  Who has just met his death,
And you assume the very shape
That makes an aged widow gape
  And robs her of her breath.

23

You make the spell-bound moon appear
To march through the all-silvered air,
    And cast through midnight's hush
Such tincture on a pallid face
A thousand-cymbaled crashing brass
    Could not restore its flush.

The terror of us all, we fear
Your hateful practice, and we bar
    Your presence from our door,
Afraid you will inflict a pox
Upon our persons, herds and flocks,
    With juice of hellebore.

Often I've watched as you espy
From far away with baleful eye
    Some shepherd on his heights;
Soon after, victim of your arts,
The man is dead, his fleshly parts
    A nest of parasites.

And yet like vile Medea, you
Could sometimes prove life-giving, too;
    You know what secret thing
Gave Aeson back his sapling youth,
Yet by your spells you have in truth
    Deprived me of my spring.

O Gods, if pity dwells on high,
May her requital be to die,
    And may her last repose,
Unblessed by burial, serve as feast
To every gross and shameful beast,
    To jackals and to crows.

(FROM PIERRE DE RONSARD)

AUSPICES

Cold, blustery cider weather, the flat fields
Bleached pale as straw, the leaves, such as remain,
Pumpkin or leather-brown. These are the wilds
Of loneliness, huge, vacant, sour and plain.

The sky is hourless dusk, portending rain.
Or perhaps snow. This narrow footpath edges
A small stand of scrub pine, warped as with pain,
And baneberry lofts its little poisoned pledges.

The footpath ends in a dried waterhole,
Plastered with black like old tar-paper siding.
The fearfullest desolations of the soul
Image themselves as local and abiding.

Even if I should get away from here
My trouser legs are stuck with burrs and seeds,
Grappled and spiked reminders of my fear,
Standing alone among the beggarweeds.

APPLICATION FOR A GRANT

Noble executors of the munificent testament
Of the late John Simon Guggenheim, distinguished bunch
Of benefactors, there are certain kinds of men
Who set their hearts on being bartenders,
For whom a life upon duck-boards, among fifths,
Tapped kegs and lemon twists, crowded with lushes
Who can master neither their bladders nor consonants,
Is the only life, greatly to be desired.
There's the man who yearns for the White House, there to
    compose
Rhythmical lists of enemies, while someone else
Wants to be known to the *Tour d'Argent's* head waiter.
As the Sibyl of Cumae said : It takes all kinds.
Nothing could bribe your Timon, your charter member
Of the Fraternal Order of Grizzly Bears to love
His fellow, whereas it's just the opposite
With interior decorators; that's what makes horse races.
One man may have a sharp nose for tax shelters,
Screwing the IRS with mirth and profit;
Another devote himself to his shell collection,
Deaf to his offspring, indifferent to the feast
With which his wife hopes to attract his notice.
Some at the Health Club sweating under bar bells
Labor away like grunting troglodytes,
Smelly and thick and inarticulate,
Their brains squeezed out through their pores by sheer
    exertion.
As for me, the prize for poets, the simple gift
For amphybrachs strewn by a kind Euterpe,
With perhaps a laurel crown of the evergreen
Imperishable of your fine endowment
Would supply my modest wants, who dream of nothing
But a pad on Eighth Street and your approbation.

(FREELY FROM HORACE)

AN OVERVIEW

Here, god-like, in a 707,
As on an air-conditioned cloud,
One knows the frailties of the proud
And comprehends the Fall from Heaven.

The world, its highways, trees and ports,
Looks much as if it were designed
With nifty model trains in mind
By salesmen at F. A. O. Schwarz.

Such the enchantment distance lends.
The bridges, matchstick and minute,
Seem faultless, intricate and cute,
Contrived for slight, aesthetic ends.

No wonder the camaraderie
Of mission-happy Air Force boys
Above so vast a spread of toys,
Cruising the skies, lighthearted, free,

Or the engaging roguishness
With which a youthful bombardier
Unloads his eggs on what appear
The perfect patchwork squares of chess;

Nor that the brass hat general staff,
Tailored and polished to a fault,
Favor an undeclared assault
On what an aerial photograph

Shows as an unstrung ball of twine,
Or that the President insist
A nation colored amethyst
Should bow to his supreme design.

But in the toy store, right up close,
Chipped paint and mucilage represent
The wounded, orphaned, indigent,
The dying and the comatose.

STILL LIFE

Sleep-walking vapor, like a visitant ghost,
      Hovers above a lake
Of Tennysonian calm just before dawn.
Inverted trees and boulders waver and coast
In polished darkness. Glints of silver break
Among the liquid leafage, and then are gone.

Everything's doused and diamonded with wet.
      A cobweb, woven taut
On bending stanchion frames of tentpole grass,
Sags like a trampoline or firemen's net
With all the glitter and riches it has caught,
Each drop a paperweight of Steuben glass.

No birdsong yet, no cricket, nor does the trout
      Explode in water-scrolls
For a skimming fly. All that is yet to come.
Things are as still and motionless throughout
The universe as ancient Chinese bowls,
And nature is magnificently dumb.

Why does this so much stir me, like a code
      Or muffled intimation
Of purposes and preordained events?
It knows me, and I recognize its mode
Of cautionary, spring-tight hesitation,
This silence so impacted and intense.

As in a water-surface I behold
      The first, soft, peach decree
Of light, its pale, inaudible commands.
I stand beneath a pine-tree in the cold,
Just before dawn, somewhere in Germany,
A cold, wet, Garand rifle in my hands.

PERSISTENCES

The leafless trees are feathery,
   A foxed, Victorian lace,
Against a sky of milk-glass blue,
   Blank, washed-out, commonplace.

Between them and my window
   Huge helices of snow
Perform their savage, churning rites
   At seventeen below.

The obscurity resembles
   A silken Chinese mist
Wherein through calligraphic daubs
   Of artistry persist

Pocked and volcanic gorges,
   Clenched and arthritic pines,
Faint, coral-tinted herons' legs
   Splashing among the tines

Of waving, tasselled marshgrass,
   Deep pools aflash with sharp,
Shingled and burnished armor-plate
   Of sacred, child-eyed carp.

This dimness is dynastic,
   An ashen T'ang of age
Or blur that grudgingly reveals
   A ghostly equipage,

Ancestral deputations
   Wound in the whited air,
To whom some sentry flings a slight,
   Prescriptive, "Who goes there?"

Are these the apparitions
    Of enemies or friends?
Loved ones from whom I once withheld
    Kindnesses or amends

On preterite occasions
    Now lost beyond repeal?
Or the old childhood torturers
    Of undiminished zeal,

Adults who ridiculed me,
    Schoolmates who broke my nose,
Risen from black, unconscious depths
    Of REM repose?

Who comes here seeking justice,
    Or in its high despite,
Bent on some hopeless interview
    On wrongs nothing can right?

Those throngs disdain to answer,
    Though numberless as flakes;
Mine is the task to find out words
    For their memorial sakes

Who press in dense approaches,
    Blue numeral tattoos
Writ crosswise on their arteries,
    The burning, voiceless Jews.

A CAST OF LIGHT

at a Father's Day picnic

A maple bough of web-foot, golden greens,
      Found by an angled shaft
Of late sunlight, disposed within that shed
Radiance, with brilliant, hoisted baldachins,
Pup tents and canopies by some underdraft
Flung up to scattered perches overhead,

These daubs of sourball lime, at floating rest,
      Present to the loose wattage
Of heaven their limelit flukes, an artifice
Of archipelagian Islands of the Blessed,
And in all innocence pursue their cottage
Industry of photosynthesis.

Yet only for twenty minutes or so today,
      On a summer afternoon,
Does the splendid lancet reach to them, or sink
To these dim bottoms, making its chancy way,
As through the barrier reef of some lagoon
In sea-green darkness, by a wavering chink,

Down, neatly probing like an accurate paw
      Or a notched and beveled key,
Through the huge cave-roof of giant oak and pine.
And the heart goes numb in a tide of fear and awe
For those we cherish, their hopes, their frailty,
Their shadowy fate's unfathomable design.

HOUSE SPARROWS

for Joe and U. T. Summers

Not of the wealthy, Coral Gables class
Of travelers, nor that rarified tax bracket,
These birds weathered the brutal, wind-chill facts
Under our eaves, nesting in withered grass,
Wormless but hopeful, and now their voice enacts
Forsythian spring with primavernal racket.

Their color is the elderly, moleskin gray
Of doggedness, of mist, magnolia bark.
Salt of the earth, they are; the common clay;
Meek *émigrés* come over on the Ark
In steerage from the Old Country of the Drowned
To settle down along Long Island Sound,

Flatbush, Weehawken, our brownstone tenements,
Wherever the local idiom is *Cheep*.
Savers of string, meticulous and mild,
They are given to nervous flight, the troubled sleep
Of those who remember terrible events,
The wide-eyed, anxious haste of the exiled.

Like all the poor, their safety lies in numbers
And hardihood and anonymity
In a world of dripping browns and duns and umbers.
They have inherited the lower sky,
Their Lake of Constants, their blue modality
That they are borne upon and battered by.

Those little shin-bones, hollow at the core,
Emaciate finger-joints, those fleshless wrists,
Wrapped in a wrinkled, loose, rice-paper skin,
As though the harvests of earth had never been,
Where have we seen such frailty before?
In pictures of Biafra and Auschwitz.

Yet here they are, these chipper stratoliners,
Unsullen, unresentful, full of the grace
Of cheerfulness, who seem to greet all comers
With the wild confidence of Forty-Niners,
And, to the lively honor of their race,
Rude canticles of "Summers, Summers, Summers."

AN OLD MALEDICTION

What well-heeled knuckle-head, straight from the unisex
Hairstylist and bathed in *Russian Leather*,
Dallies with you these late summer days, Pyrrha,
In your expensive sublet? For whom do you
Slip into something simple by, say, Gucci?
The more fool he who has mapped out for himself
The saline latitudes of incontinent grief.
Dazzled though he be, poor dope, by the golden looks
Your locks fetched up out of a bottle of *Clairol*,
He will know that the wind changes, the smooth sailing
Is done for, when the breakers wallop him broadside,
When he's rudderless, dismasted, thoroughly swamped
In that mindless rip-tide that got the best of me
Once, when I ventured on your deeps, Piranha.

(FREELY FROM HORACE)

II

THE VENETIAN VESPERS

for Harry and Kathleen Ford

> . . *where's that palace whereinto foul things*
> *Sometimes intrude not? Who has a breast so pure*
> *But some uncleanly apprehensions*
> *Keep leets and law days, and in session sit*
> *With meditations lawful?*
>> Othello: III, iii, 136–41

> *We cannot all have our gardens now, nor our*
> *pleasant fields to meditate in at eventide.*
>> RUSKIN: *The Stones of Venice,*
>> BK. I, CH. XXX

I

What's merciful is not knowing where you are,
What time it is, even your name or age,
But merely a clean coolness at the temple—
That, says the spirit softly, is enough
For the mind to adventure on its half-hidden path
Like starlight interrupted by dense trees
Journeying backwards on a winter trip
While you are going, as you fancy, forward,
And the stars are keeping pace with everything.
Where to begin? With the white, wrinkled membrane,
The disgusting skin that gathers on hot milk?
Or narrow slabs of jasper light at sundown
That fit themselves softly around the legs
Of chairs, and entertain a drift of motes,
A tide of sadness, a failing, a dying fall?
Or the glass jar, like a dry cell battery,
Full of electric coils and boiling resins,
Its tin Pinocchio nose with one small nostril,
And both of us under a tent of towels

Like child conspirators, the tin nose breathing
Health at me steadily, like the insufflation of God?
Yes, but also the sight, on a gray morning,
Beneath the crossbar of an iron railing
Painted a glossy black, of six waterdrops
Slung in suspension, sucking into themselves,
As if it were some morbid nourishment,
The sagging blackness of the rail itself,
But edged with brilliant fingernails of chrome
In which the world was wonderfully disfigured
Like faces seen in spoons, like mirrorings
In the fine spawn, the roe of air bubbles,
That tiny silver wampum along the stems,
Yellowed and magnified, of aging flowers
Caught in the lens of stale water and glass
In the upstairs room when somebody had died.
Just like the beads they sprinkled over cookies
At Christmas. Or perhaps those secret faces
Known to no one but me, slyly revealed
In repetitions of the wallpaper,
My tight network of agents in the field.
Well, yes. Any of these might somehow serve
As a departure point. But, perhaps, best
Would be those first precocious hints of hell,
Those intuitions of living desolation
That last a lifetime. These were never, for me,
Some desert place that humans had avoided
In which I could get lost, to which I might
In dreams condemn myself—a wilderness
Natural but alien and unpitying.
They were instead those derelict waste places
Abandoned by mankind as of no worth,
Frequented, if at all, by the dispossessed,
Nocturnal shapes, the crippled and the shamed.
Here in the haywire weeds, concealed by wilds
Of goldenrod and toadflax, lies a spur
With its one boxcar of brick-colored armor,

At noon, midsummer, fiercer than a kiln,
Rippling the thinness of the air around it
With visible distortions. Among the stones
Of the railbed, fragments of shattered amber
That held a pint of rye. The carapace
Of a dried beetle. A broken orange crate
Streaked with tobacco stains at the nailheads
In the gray, fractured slats. And over all
The dust of oblivion finer than milled flour
Where chips of brick, clinkers and old iron
Burn in their slow, invisible decay.
Or else it is late afternoon in autumn,
The sunlight rusting on the western fronts
Of a long block of Victorian brick houses,
Untenanted, presumably condemned,
Their brownstone grapes, their grand entablatures,
Their straining caryatid muscle-men
Rendered at once ridiculous and sad
By the black scars of zigzag fire escapes
That double themselves in isometric shadows.
And all their vacancy is given voice
By the endless flapping of one window-shade.
And then there is the rank, familiar smell
Of underpasses, the dark piers of bridges,
Where old men, the incontinent, urinate.
The acid smell of poverty, the jest
Of adolescent boys exchanging quips
About bedpans, the motorman's comfort,
A hospital world of syphons and thick tubes
That they know nothing of. Nor do they know
The heatless burnings of the elderly
In memorized, imaginary lusts,
Visions of noontide infidelities,
Crude hallway gropings, cruel lubricities,
A fire as cold and slow as rusting metal.
It's but a child's step, it's but an old man's totter
From this to the appalling world of dreams.

Gray bottled babies in formaldehyde
As in their primal amniotic bath.
Pale dowagers hiding their liver-spots
In a fine chalk, confectionery dust.
And then the unbearable close-up of a wart
With a tough bristle of hair, like a small beast
With head and feet tucked under, playing possum.
A meat-hooked ham, hung like a traitor's head
For the public's notice in a butcher shop,
Faintly resembling the gartered thigh
Of an acrobatic, overweight soubrette.
And a scaled, crusted animal whose head
Fits in a Nazi helmet, whose webbed feet
Are cold on the white flanks of dreaming lovers,
While thorned and furry legs embrace each other
As black mandibles tick. Immature girls,
Naked but for the stockings they stretch tight
To tempt the mucid glitter of an eye.
And the truncated snout of a small bat,
Like one whose nose, undermined by the pox,
Falls back to the skull's socket. Deepest of all,
Like the converging lines in diagrams
Of vanishing points, those underwater blades,
Those quills or sunburst spokes of marine light,
Flutings and gilded shafts in which one sees
In the drowned star of intersecting beams
Just at that final moment of suffocation
The terrifying and unmeaning rictus
Of the sandshark's stretched, involuntary grin.
In the upstairs room, when somebody had died,
There were flowers, there were underwater globes,
Mercury seedpearls. It was my mother died.
After a long illness and long ago.

    San Pantaleone, heavenly buffoon,
Patron of dotards and of gondolas,
Forgive us the obsessional daydream

Of our redemption at work in black and white,
The silent movie, the old *Commedia*,
Which for the sake of the children in the house
The projectionist has ventured to run backwards.
(The reels must be rewound in any case.)
It is because of jumped, elided frames
That people make their way by jigs and spasms,
Impetuous leapings, violent semaphores,
Side-slipping, drunk discontinuities,
Like the staggered, tossed career of butterflies.
Here, in pure satisfaction of our hunger,
The Keystone Cops sprint from hysteria,
From brisk, slaphappy bludgeonings of crime,
Faultlessly backwards into calm patrol;
And gallons of spilled paint, meekly obedient
As a domestic pet, home in and settle
Securely into casually offered pails,
Leaving the Persian rugs immaculate.
But best of all are the magically dry legs
Emerging from a sudden crater of water
That closes itself up like a healed wound
To plate-glass polish as the diver slides
Upwards, attaining with careless arrogance
His unsought footing on the highest board.
Something profoundly soiled, pointlessly hurt
And beyond cure in us yearns for this costless
Ablution, this impossible reprieve,
Unpurchased at a scaffold, free, bequeathed
As rain upon the just and the unjust,
As in the fall of mercy, unconstrained,
Upon the poor, infected place beneath.

II

Elsewhere the spirit is summoned back to life
By bells sifted through floating schools and splices
Of sun-splashed poplar leaves, a reverie
Of light chromatics (Monet and Debussy),
Or the intemperate storms and squalls of traffic,
The coarse, unanswered voice of a fog horn,
Or, best, the shy, experimental aubade
Of the first birds to sense that ashen cold
Grisaille from which the phoenix dawn arises.
Summoned, that is to say, to the world's life
From Piranesian *Carceri* and rat holes
Of its own deep contriving. But here in Venice,
The world's most louche and artificial city,
(In which my tale some time will peter out)
The summons comes from the harsh smashing of glass.
A not unsuitable local industry,
Being the frugal and space-saving work
Of the young men who run the garbage scows.
Wine bottles of a clear sea-water green,
Pale, smoky quarts of *acqua minerale*,
Iodine-tinted liters, the true-blue
Waterman's midnight ink of Bromo Seltzer,
Light-bulbs of packaged fog, fluorescent tubes
Of well-sealed, antiseptic samples of cloud,
Await what is at once their liquidation
And resurrection in the glory holes
Of the Murano furnaces. Meanwhile
Space must be made for all ephemera,
Our cast-offs, foulings, whatever has gone soft
With age, or age has hardened to a stone,
Our city sweepings. Venice has no curbs
At which to curb a dog, so underfoot
The ochre pastes and puddings of dogshit
Keep us earthbound in half a dozen ways,
Curbing the spirit's tendency to pride.

The palaces decay. Venice is rich
Chiefly in the deposits of her dogs.
A wealth swept up and gathered with its makers.
Canaries, mutts, love-birds and alley cats
Are sacked away like so many Monte Cristos,
There being neither lawns, meadows nor hillsides
To fertilize or to be buried in.
For them the glass is broken in the dark
As a remembrance by the garbage men.
I am their mourner at collection time
With an invented litany of my own.
Wagner died here, Stravinsky's buried here,
They say that Cimarosa's enemies
Poisoned him here. The mind at four AM
Is a poor, blotched, vermiculated thing.
I've seen it spilled like sweetbreads, and I've dreamed
Of Byron writing, "Many a fine day
I should have blown my brains out but for the thought
Of the pleasure it would give my mother-in-law."
Thus virtues, it is said, are forced upon us
By our own impudent crimes. I think of him
With his consorts of whores and countesses
Smelling of animal musk, lilac and garlic,
A *ménage* that was in fact a menagerie,
A fox, a wolf, a mastiff, birds and monkeys,
Corbaccios and corvinos, *spintriae*,
The lees of the Venetian underworld,
A plague of iridescent flies. Spilled out.
O lights and livers. Deader than dead weight.
In a casket lined with tufted tea-rose silk.
O that the soul should tie its shoes, the mind
Should wash its hands in a sink, that a small grain
Of immortality should fit itself
With dentures. We slip down by grades and degrees,
Lapses of memory, the vacant eye
And spittled lip, by soiled humiliations
Of mind and body into the last ditch,

Passing, en route to the *Incurabili,*
The backwater way stations of the soul,
Conveyed in the glossy hearse-and-coffin black
And soundless gondola by an overpriced
Apprentice Charon to the *Calle dei Morti.*
One approaches the Venetian underworld
Silently and by water, the gondolier
Creating eddies and whirlpools with each stroke
Like oak roots, silver, smooth and muscular.
One slides to it like a swoon, nearing the regions
Where the vast hosts of the dead mutely inhabit,
Pulseless, indifferent, deeply beyond caring
What shape intrudes itself upon their fathoms.
The oar-blade flings broadcast its beads of light,
Its ordinary gems. One travels past
All of these domiciles of raw sienna,
Burnt umber, colors of the whole world's clays.
One's weakness in itself becomes delicious
Towards the end, a kindly vacancy.
(Raise both your arms above your head, and then
Take three deep breaths, holding the third. Your partner,
Your childhood guide into the other world,
Will approach from behind and wrap you in a bear hug,
Squeezing with all his might. Your head will seethe
With prickled numbness, like an arm or leg
From which the circulation is cut off,
The lungs turn warm with pain, and then you slip
Into a velvet darkness, mutely grateful
To your Anubis-executioner . . .)
Probably I shall die here unremarked
Amid the albergo's seedy furniture,
Aware to the last of the faintly rotten scent
Of swamp and sea, a brief embarrassment
And nuisance to the management and the maid.
That would be bad enough without the fear
Byron confessed to : "If I should reach old age
I'll die 'at the top first,' like Swift." Or Swift's

Lightning-struck tree. There was a visitor,
The little Swiss authority on nightmares,
Young Henry Fuseli, who at thirty-one
Suffered a fever here for several days
From which he recovered with his hair turned white
As a judicial wig, and rendered permanently
Left-handed. And His Majesty, George III,
Desired the better acquaintance of a tree
At Windsor, and heartily shook one of its branches,
Taking it for the King of Prussia. Laugh
Whoso will that has no knowledge of
The violent ward. They subdued that one
With a hypodermic, quickly tranquilized
And trussed him like a fowl. These days I find
A small aperitif at Florian's
Is helpful, although I do not forget.
My views are much like Fuseli's, who described
His method thus: "I first sits myself down.
I then works myself up. Then I throws in
My darks. And then I takes away my lights."
His nightmare was a great success, while mine
Plays on the ceiling of my rented room
Or on the bone concavity of my skull
In the dark hours when I take away my lights.

      Lights. I have chosen Venice for its light,
Its lightness, buoyancy, its calm suspension
In time and water, its strange quietness.
I, an expatriate American,
Living off an annuity, confront
The lagoon's waters in mid-morning sun.
Palladio's church floats at its anchored peace
Across from me, and the great church of Health,
Voted in gratitude by the Venetians
For heavenly deliverance from the plague,
Voluted, levels itself on the canal.
Further away the bevels coil and join

Like spiraled cordon ropes of silk, the lips
Of the crimped water sped by a light breeze.
Morning has tooled the bay with bright inlays
Of writhing silver, scattered scintillance.
These little crests and ripples promenade,
Hurried and jocular and never bored,
Ils se promènent like families of some means
On Sundays in the *Bois*. Observing this
Easy festivity, hypnotized by
Tiny sun-signals exchanged across the harbor,
I am for the moment cured of everything,
The future held at bay, the past submerged,
Even the fact that this Sea of Hadria,
This consecrated, cool wife of the Doge,
Was ploughed by the merchantmen of all the world,
And all the silicate fragility
They sweat for at the furnaces now seems
An admirable and shatterable triumph.
They take the first crude bulb of thickened glass,
Glowing and taffy-soft on the blow tube,
And sink it in a mold, a metal cup
Spiked on its inner surface like a pineapple.
Half the glass now is regularly dimpled,
And when these dimples are covered with a glaze
Of molten glass they are prisoned air-bubbles,
Breathless, enameled pearly vacancies.

III

I am a person of inflexible habits
And comforting rigidities, and though
I am a twentieth century infidel
From Lawrence, Massachusetts, twice a week
I visit the Cathedral of St. Mark's,
That splendid monument to the labors of
Grave robbers, body snatchers, those lawless two
Entrepreneurial Venetians who
In compliance with the wishes of the Doge
For the greater commercial and religious glory
Of Venice in the year 828
Kidnapped the corpse of the Evangelist
From Alexandria, a sacrilege
The saint seemed to approve. That ancient city
Was drugged and bewildered with an odor of sanctity,
Left powerless and mystified by oils,
Attars and essences of holiness
And roses during the midnight exhumation
And spiriting away of the dead saint
By Buono and his side-kick Rustico—
Goodness in concert with Simplicity
Effecting the major heist of Christendom.

I enter the obscure aquarium dimness,
The movie-palace dark, through which incline
Smoky diagonals and radiant bars
Of sunlight from the high southeastern crescents
Of windowed drums above. Like slow blind fingers
Finding their patient and unvarying way
Across the braille of pavement, edging along
The pavonine and lapidary walls,
Inching through silence as the earth revolves
To huge compulsions, as the turning spheres
Drift in their milky pale galactic light
Through endless quiet, gigantic vacancy,

Unpitying, inhuman, terrible.
In time the eye accommodates itself
To the dull phosphorescence. Gradually
Glories reveal themselves, grave mysteries
Of the faith cast off their shadows, assume their forms
Against a heaven of coined and sequined light,
A splatter of gilt cobblestones, flung grains
Or crumbs of brilliance, the vast open fields
Of the sky turned intimate and friendly. Patines
And laminae, a vermeil shimmering
Of fish-scaled, cataphracted golden plates.
Here are the saints and angels brought together
In studied reveries of happiness.
Enormous wings of seraphim uphold
The crowning domes where the convened apostles
Receive their fiery tongues from the Godhead
Descended to them as a floating dove,
Patriarch and collateral ancestor
Of the pigeons out in the Square. Into those choirs
Of lacquered Thrones, enameled Archangels
And medaled Principalities rise up
A cool plantation of columns, marble shafts
Bearing their lifted pathways, viaducts
And catwalks through the middle realms of heaven.
Even as God descended into the mass
And thick of us, so is He borne aloft
As promise and precursor to us all,
Ascending in the central dome's vast hive
Of honeyed luminosity. Behind
The altar He appears, two fingers raised
In benediction, in what seems two-thirds
Of the Boy Scout salute, wishing us well.
And we are gathered here below the saints,
Virtues and martyrs, sheltered in their glow,
Soothed by the punk and incense, to rejoice
In the warm light of Gabrieli's horns,
And for a moment of unwonted grace

We are so blessed as to forget ourselves.
Perhaps. There is something selfish in the self,
The cell's craving for perpetuity,
The sperm's ignorant hope, the animal's rule
Of haunch and sinew, testicle and groin,
That refers all things whatever, near and far,
To one's own needs or fantasized desires.
Returning suddenly to the chalk-white sunlight
Of out-of-doors, one spots among the tourists
Those dissolute young with heavy-lidded gazes
Of cool, clear-eyed, stony depravity
That in the course of only a few years
Will fade into the terrifying boredom
In the faces of Carpaccio's prostitutes.
From motives that are anything but kindly
I ignore their indiscreet solicitations
And far more obvious poverty. The mind
Can scarcely cope with the world's sufferings,
Must blinker itself to much or else go mad.
And the bargain that we make for our sanity
Is the knowledge that when at length it comes our turn
To be numbered with the outcasts, the maimed, the poor,
The injured and insulted, they will turn away,
The fortunate and healthy, as I turn now
(Though touched as much with compassion as with lust,
Knowing the smallest gift would reverse our roles,
Expose me as weak and thus exploitable.
There is more stamina, twenty times more hope
In the least of them than there is left in me.)
I take my loneliness as a vocation,
A policied exile from the human race,
A cultivated, earned misanthropy
After the fashion of the Miller of Dee.

    It wasn't always so. I was an Aid Man,
A Medic with an infantry company,
Who because of my refusal to bear arms

Was constrained to bear the wounded and the dead
From under enemy fire, and to bear witness
To inconceivable pain, usually shot at
Though banded with Red Crosses and unarmed.
There was a corporal I knew in Heavy Weapons,
Someone who carried with him into combat
A book of etiquette by Emily Post.
Most brought with them some token of the past,
Some emblem of attachment or affection
Or coddled childhood—bibles and baby booties,
Harmonicas, love letters, photographs—
But this was different. I discovered later
That he had been brought up in an orphanage,
So the book was his fiction of kindliness,
A novel in which personages of wealth
Firmly secure domestic tranquility.
He'd cite me instances. It seems a boy
Will not put "Mr." on his calling cards
Till he leaves school, and may omit the "Mr."
Even while at college. Bread and butter plates
Are never placed on a formal dinner table.
At a simple dinner party one may serve
Claret instead of champagne with the meat.
The satin facings on a butler's lapels
Are narrower than a gentleman's, and he wears
Black waistcoat with white tie, whereas the gentleman's
White waistcoat goes with both black tie and white.
When a lady lunches alone at her own home
In a formally kept house the table is set
For four. As if three Elijahs were expected.
This was to him a sort of *Corpus Juris*,
An ancient piety and governance
Worthy of constant dream and meditation.
He haunts me here, that seeker after law
In a lawless world, in rainsoaked combat boots,
Oil-stained fatigues and heavy bandoleers.
He was killed by enemy machine-gun fire.

His helmet had fallen off. They had sheared away
The top of his cranium like a soft-boiled egg,
And there he crouched, huddled over his weapon,
His brains wet in the chalice of his skull.

IV

       Where to begin? In a heaven of golden serifs
Or smooth and rounded loaves of risen gold,
Formed into formal Caslon capitals
And graced with a pretzeled, sinuous ampersand
Against a sanded ground of fire-truck red,
Proclaiming to the world at large, "The Great
Atlantic & Pacific Tea Co."?
The period alone appeared to me
An eighteen-karat doorknob beyond price.
This was my uncle's store where I was raised.
A shy asthmatic child, I was permitted
To improvise with used potato sacks
Of burlap a divan behind the counter
Where I could lie and read or dream my dreams.
These were infused with the smell of fruit and coffee,
Strong odors of American abundance.
Under the pressed-tin ceiling's coffering
I'd listen to the hissing radiator,
Hung with its can, like a tapped maple tree,
To catch its wrathful spittings, and meditate
On the arcane meaning of the mystic word
(Fixed in white letters backwards on the window)
That referred inscrutably to nothing else
Except itself. An uncracked code: SALADA.
By childhood's rules of inference it concerned
Saladin and the camphors of the East,
And through him, by some cognate lineage
Of sound and mystic pedigree, Aladdin,
A hushed and shadowy world of minarets,
Goldsmiths, persimmons and the ninety-nine
Unutterable Arabian names of God.
I had an eye for cyphers and riddling things.
Of all my schoolmates I was the only one
Who knew that on the bottle of Worcestershire
The conjured names of Lea and Perrins figure

Forty-eight times, weaving around the border
As well as the obvious places front and back.
I became in time a local spelling champion,
Encouraged and praised at home, where emphasis
Was placed on what was then called *elocution*
And upon "building" a vocabulary,
A project that seemed allied to architecture,
The unbuttressed balancing of wooden blocks
Into a Tower of Babel. Still, there were prizes
For papers in my English class: Carlyle
On The Dignity of Labor; John Stuart Mill
On Happiness. But the origin of things
Lies elsewhere. Back in some genetic swamp.

    My uncle had worked hard to get his store.
Soon as he could he brought his younger brothers
From the Old Country. My father brought his bride
Of two months to the second-story room
Above the storage. Everybody shared
Labors and profits; they stayed open late
Seven days a week (but closed on Christmas Day)
And did all right. But cutting up the pie
Of measured earnings among five adults
(Four brothers and my mother—I didn't count,
Being one year old at the time) seemed to my father
A burden upon everyone. He announced
That he was going west to make his fortune
And would send soon as he could for mother and me.
Everyone thought him brave and enterprising.
There was a little party, with songs and tears
And special wine, purchased for the occasion.
He left. We never heard from him again.

    When I was six years old it rained and rained
And never seemed to stop. I had an oilskin,
A bright sou'wester, stiff and sunflower yellow,
And fireman boots. Rain stippled the windows

Of the school bus that brought us home at dusk
That was no longer dusk but massing dark
As that small world of kids drove into winter,
And always in that dark our grocery store
Looked like a theater or a puppet show,
Lit, warm, and peopled with the family cast,
Full of prop vegetables, a brighter sight
Than anyone else's home. Therefore I knew
Something was clearly up when the bus door
Hinged open and all the lights were on upstairs
But only the bulb at the cash register lit
The store itself, half dark, and on the steps,
Still in his apron, standing in the rain,
My uncle. He was soaked through. He told me
He was taking me to a movie and then to supper
At a restaurant, though the next day was school
And I had homework. It was clear to me
That such a treat exacted on my part
The condition that I shouldn't question it.
We went to see a bedroom comedy,
"Let Us Be Gay," scarcely for six-year-olds,
Throughout the length of which my uncle wept.
And then we went to a Chinese restaurant
And sat next to the window where I could see,
Beyond the Chinese equivalent of SALADA
Encoded on the glass, the oil-slicked streets,
The gutters with their little Allagashes
Bent on some urgent mission to the sea.
Next day they told me that my mother was dead.
I didn't go to school. I watched the rain
From the bedroom window or from my burlap nest
Behind the counter. My whole life was changed
Without my having done a single thing.
Perhaps because of those days of constant rain
I am always touched by it now, touched and assuaged.
Perhaps that early vigilance at windows
Explains why I have now come to regard

Life as a spectator sport. But I find peace
In the arcaded dark of the piazza
When a thunderstorm comes up. I watch the sky
Cloud into tarnished zinc, to Quaker gray
Drabness, its shrouded vaults, fog-bound crevasses
Blinking with huddled lightning, and await
The vast *son et lumière*. The city's lamps
Faintly ignite in the gathered winter gloom.
The rumbled thunder starts—an avalanche
Rolling down polished corridors of sound,
Rickety tumbrels blundering across
A stone and empty cellarage. And then,
Like a whisper of dry leaves, the rain begins.
It stains the paving stones, forms a light mist
Of brilliant crystals dulled with tones of lead
Three inches off the ground. Blown shawls of rain
Quiver and luff, veil the cathedral front
In flailing laces while the street lamps hold
Fixed globes of sparkled haze high in the air
And the black pavement runs with wrinkled gold
In pools and wet dispersions, fiery spills
Of liquid copper, of squirming, molten brass.
To give one's whole attention to such a sight
Is a sort of blessedness. No room is left
For antecedence, inference, nuance.
One escapes from all the anguish of this world
Into the refuge of the present tense.
The past is mercifully dissolved, and in
Easy obedience to the gospel's word,
One takes no thought whatever of tomorrow,
The soul being drenched in fine particulars.

V

     Seeing is misbelieving, as may be seen
By the angled stems, like fractured tibias,
Misplaced by water's anamorphosis.
Think of the blonde with the exposed midriff
Who grins as the cross-cut saw slides through her navel,
Or, better, the wobbled clarity of streams,
Their graveled bottoms strewn with casual plunder
Of earthen golds, shark grays, palomino browns
Giddily swimming in and out of focus,
Where, in a passing moment of accession,
One thinks one sees in all that spangled bath,
That tarsial, cosmatesque bespattering,
The anchored floating of a giant trout.
All lenses—the corneal tunic of the eye,
Fine scopes and glazier's filaments—mislead us
With insubstantial visions, like objects viewed
Through crizzled and quarrelled panes of Bull's Eye Glass.
It turned out in the end that John Stuart Mill
Knew even less about happiness than I do,
Who know at last, alas, that it is composed
Of clouded, cataracted, darkened sight,
Merciful blindnesses and ignorance.
Only when paradisal bliss had ended
Was enlightenment vouchsafed to Adam and Eve,
"*And the eyes of them both were opened, and they knew . . .*"
I, for example, though I had lost my parents,
Thought I was happy almost throughout my youth.
Innocent, like Othello in his First Act.
"*I saw 't not, thought it not, it harmed not me.*"
The story I have to tell is only my story
By courtesy of painful inference.
So far as I can tell it, it is true,
Though it has comprised the body of such dreams,
Such broken remnant furnishings of the mind
That my unwilling suspension of disbelief

No longer can distinguish between fact
As something outward, independent, given,
And the enfleshment of disembodied thought,
Some melanotic malevolence of my own.
I know this much for sure: When I was eighteen
My father returned home. In a boxcar, dead.
I learned, or else I dreamed, that heading west
He got no further than Toledo, Ohio,
Where late one night in a vacant parking lot
He was robbed, hit on the head with a quart bottle,
Left bleeding and unconscious and soaked with rum
By a couple of thugs who had robbed a liquor store
And found in my father, besides his modest savings,
A convenient means of diverting the police.
He came to in the hospital, walletless,
Paperless, without identity.
He had no more than a dozen words of English
Which, in hysterical anxiety
Or perhaps from the concussion, evaded him.
The doctors seemed to be equally alarmed
By possible effects of the blow to his head
And by his wild excitability
In a tongue nobody there could understand.
He was therefore transferred for observation
To the State Mental Hospital where he stayed
Almost a year before, by merest chance,
A visitor of Lithuanian background
Heard and identified his Lettish speech,
And it could be determined that he was
In full possession of his faculties,
If of little else, and where he had come from
And all the rest of it. The Toledo police
Then wrote my uncle a letter. Without unduly
Stressing their own casualness in the matter,
They told my uncle where his brother was,
How he had come to be there, and that because
He had no funds or visible means of support

He would be held pending a money order
That should cover at least his transportation home.
They wrote three times. They didn't get an answer.

　　　The immigrants to Lawrence, Massachusetts,
Were moved as by the vision of Isaiah
To come to the New World, to become new
And enter into a peaceful Commonwealth.
This meant hard work, a scrupulous adoption
Of local ways, endeavoring to please
Clients and neighbors, to become at length,
Despite the ineradicable stigma
Of a thick accent, one like all the rest,
Homogenized and inconspicuous.
So much had the prophetic vision come to.
It would not do at all to have it known
That any member of the family
Had been in police custody, or, worse,
In an asylum. All the kind good will
And friendly custom of the neighborhood
Would be withdrawn at the mere breath of scandal.
Prudence is one of the New England virtues
My uncle was at special pains to learn.
And it paid off, as protestant virtue does,
In cold coin of the realm. Soon he could buy
His own store and take his customers with him
From the A. & P. By the time I was in high school
He and his brothers owned a modest chain
Of little grocery stores and butcher shops.
And he took on as well the unpaid task
Of raising me, making himself my parent,
Forbearing and encouraging and kind.
Or so it seemed. Often in my nightmares
Since then I appear craven and repulsive,
Always soliciting his good opinion
As he had sought that of the neighborhood.
The dead keep their own counsel, let nothing slip

About incarceration, so it was judged
Fitting to have the funeral back home.
Home now had changed. We lived, uncle and I,
In a whole house of our own with a German cook.
The body was laid out in the living room
In a casket lined with tufted tea-rose silk,
Upholstered like a Victorian love-seat.
He had never been so comfortable. He looked
Almost my age, more my age than my uncle's,
Since half his forty years had not been lived,
Had merely passed, like birthdays or the weather.
He was, strangely enough, a total stranger
Who bore a clear family resemblance.
And there was torture in my uncle's face
Such as I did not even see at war.
The flowers were suffocating. It was like drowning.
The day after the burial I enlisted,
And two and a half years later was mustered out
As a Section Eight, mentally unsound.

VI

What is our happiest, most cherished dream
Of paradise? Not harps and fugues and feathers
But rather arrested action, an escape
From time, from history, from evolution
Into the blessèd stasis of a painting :
Those tributes, homages, apotheoses
Figured upon the ceilings of the rich
Wherein some rather boorish-looking count,
With game leg and bad breath, roundly despised
By all of his contemporaries, rises
Into the company of the heavenly host
(A pimpled donor among flawless saints)
Viewed by us proletarians on the floor
From under his thick ham and dangled calf
As he is borne beyond our dark resentment
On puffy quilts and comforters of cloud.
Suspended always at that middle height
In numinous diffusions of soft light,
In mild soft-focus, in the "tinted steam"
Of Turner's visions of reality,
He is established at a pitch of triumph,
That shall not fail him, by the painter's skill.
Yet in its way even the passage of time
Seems to inch toward a vast and final form,
To mimic the grand metastasis of art,
As if all were ordained. As the writ saith :
The fathers (and their brothers) shall eat grapes
And the teeth of the children shall be set on edge.
Ho fatto un fiasco, which is to say,
I've made a sort of bottle of my life,
A frangible and a transparent failure.
My efforts at their best are negative :
A poor attempt not to hurt anyone,
A goal which, in the very nature of things,
Is ludicrous because impossible.

Viscid, contaminate, dynastic wastes
Flood through the dark canals, the underpasses,
Ducts and arterial sluices of my body
As through those gutters of which Swift once wrote:
"Sweepings from Butcher Stalls, Dung, Guts, and Blood,
Drown'd Puppies, stinking Sprats, all drench'd in Mud,
Dead Cats and Turnip-Tops come tumbling down the
     Flood."
At least I pass them on to nobody,
Not having married, or authored any children,
Leading a monkish life of modest means
On a trust fund established by my uncle
In a will of which I am the single heir.
I am not young any more, and not very well,
Subject to nightmares and to certain fevers
The doctors cannot cure. There's a Madonna
Set in an alley shrine near where I live
Whose niche is filled with little votive gifts,
Like cookie molds, of pressed tin eyes and legs
And organs she has mercifully cured.
She is not pretty, she is not high art,
But in my infidel way I'm fond of her—
Saint Mary Paregoric, Comforter.
Were she to cure me, what could I offer her?
The gross, intestinal wormings of the brain?

     A virus's life-span is twenty minutes.
Think of its evolutionary zeal,
Like the hyper-active balance-wheel of a watch,
Busy with swift mutations, trundling through
Its own Silurian epochs in a week;
By fierce ambition and Darwinian wit
Acquiring its immunities against
Our warfares and our plagues of medication.
Blessed be the unseen micro-organisms,
For without doubt they shall inherit the earth.
Their generations shall be as the sands of the sea.

I am the dying host by which they live;
In me they dwell and thrive and have their being.
I am the tapered end of a long line,
The thin and febrile phylum of my family :
Of all my father's brothers the one child.
I wander these by-paths and little squares,
A singular Tyrannosauros Rex,
Sauntering towards extinction, an obsolete
Left-over from a weak *ancien régime*
About to be edged out by upstart germs.
I shall pay out the forfeit with my life
In my own lingering way. Just as my uncle,
Who, my blood tells me on its nightly rounds,
May perhaps be "a little more than kin,"
Has paid the price for his unlawful grief
And bloodless butchery by creating me
His guilty legatee, the beneficiary
Of his money and his crimes.
                              In these late days
I find myself frequently at the window,
Its glass a cooling comfort to my temple.
And I lift up mine eyes, not to the hills
Of which there are not any, but to the clouds.
Here is a sky determined to maintain
The reputation of Tiepolo,
A moving vision of a shapely mist,
Full of the splendor of the insubstantial.
Against a diorama of palest blue
Cloud-curds, cloud-stacks, cloud-bushes sun themselves.
Giant confections, impossible meringues,
Soft coral reefs and powdery tumuli
Pass in august processions and calm herds.
Great stadiums, grandstands and amphitheaters,
The tufted, opulent litters of the gods
They seem; or laundered bunting, well-dressed wigs,
Harvests of milk-white, Chinese peonies
That visibly rebuke our stinginess.

For all their ghostly presences, they take on
A colorful nobility at evening.
Off to the east the sky begins to turn
Lilac so pale it seems a mood of gray,
Gradually, like the death of virtuous men.
Streaks of electrum richly underline
The slow, flat-bottomed hulls, those floated lobes
Between which quills and spokes of light fan out
Into carnelian reds and nectarines,
Nearing a citron brilliance at the center,
The searing furnace of the glory hole
That fires and fuses clouds of muscatel
With pencilings of gold. I look and look,
As though I could be saved simply by looking—
I, who have never earned my way, who am
No better than a viral parasite,
Or the lees of the Venetian underworld,
Foolish and muddled in my later years,
Who was never even at one time a wise child.

III

TWO POEMS BY JOSEPH BRODSKY

VERSIONS BY ANTHONY HECHT

CAPE COD LULLABY

I

The Eastern tip of the Empire dives into night;
Cicadas fall silent over some empty lawn;
On classic pediments inscriptions dim from the sight
As a finial cross darkens and then is gone
Like the nearly empty bottle on the table.
From the empty street's patrol-car a refrain
Of Ray Charles' keyboard tinkles away like rain.

Crawling to a vacant beach from the vast wet
Of ocean, a crab digs into sand laced with sea-lather
And sleeps. A giant clock on a brick tower
Rattles its scissors. The face is drenched with sweat.
The street lamps glisten in the stifling weather,
Formally spaced,
Like white shirt buttons open to the waist.

It's stifling. The eye's guided by a blinking stop-light
In its journey to the whiskey across the room
On the night-stand. The heart stops dead a moment, but its
    dull boom
Goes on, and the blood, on pilgrimage gone forth,
Comes back to a crossroad. The body, like an upright,
Rolled-up road-map, lifts an eyebrow in the North.

It's strange to think of surviving, but that's what happened.
Dust settles on furnishings, and a car bends length
Around corners in spite of Euclid. And the deepened
Darkness makes up for the absence of people, of voices,
And so forth, and alters them, by its cunning and strength,
Not to deserters, to ones who have taken flight,
But rather to those now disappeared from sight.

It's stifling. And the thick leaves' rasping sound
Is enough all by itself to make you sweat.
What seems to be a small dot in the dark
Could only be one thing—a star. On the deserted ground
Of a basketball court a vagrant bird has set
Its fragile egg in the steel hoop's ravelled net.
There's a smell of mint now, and of mignonette.

II

Like a despotic Sheik, who can be untrue
To his vast seraglio and multiple desires
Only with a harem altogether new,
Varied and numerous, I have switched Empires.
A step dictated by the acrid, live
Odor of burning carried on the air
From all four quarters (a time for silent prayer!)
And, from the crow's high vantage point, from five.

Like a snake charmer, like the Pied Piper of old,
Playing my flute I passed the green janissaries,
My testes sensing their pole axe's sinister cold,
As when one wades into water. And then with the brine
Of sea-water sharpness filling, flooding the mouth,
I crossed the line

And sailed into muttony clouds. Below me curled
Serpentine rivers, roads bloomed with dust, ricks yellowed,
And everywhere in that diminished world,
In formal opposition, near and far,
Lined up like print in a book about to close,
Armies rehearsed their games in balanced rows
And cities all went dark as caviar.

And then the darkness thickened. All lights fled,
A turbine droned, a head ached rhythmically,
And space backed up like a crab, time surged ahead
Into first place, and streaming westwardly,
Seemed to be heading home, void of all light,
Soiling its garments with the tar of night.

I fell asleep. When I awoke to the day,
Magnetic north had strengthened its deadly pull.
I beheld new heavens, I beheld the earth made new.
It lay
Turning to dust, as flat things always do.

III

Being itself the essence of all things,
Solitude teaches essentials. How gratefully the skin
Receives the leathery coolness of its chair.
Meanwhile my arm, off in the dark somewhere,
Goes wooden in sympathetic brotherhood
With the chair's listless arm of oaken wood.
A glowing oaken grain
Covers the tiny bones of the joints. And the brain
Knocks like the glass's ice-cube tinkling.

It's stifling. On a pool hall's steps, in a dim glow,
Somebody striking a match rescues his face
Of an old black man from the enfolding dark
For a flaring moment. The white-toothed portico
Of the District Courthouse sinks in the thickened lace
Of foliage, and awaits the random search
Of passing headlights. High up on its perch,

Like the fiery warning at Belshazzar's Feast,
The inscription, *Coca-Cola*, hums in red.
In the Country Club's unweeded flowerbed
A fountain whispers its secrets. Unable to rouse
A simple *tirra lirra* in these dull boughs,
A strengthless breeze rustles the tattered, creased
News of the world, its obsolete events,
Against an improvised, unlikely fence

Of iron bedsteads. It's stifling. Leaning on his rifle,
The Unknown Soldier grows even more unknown.
Against a concrete jetty, in dull repose
A trawler scrapes the rusty bridge of its nose.
A weary, buzzing ventilator mills
The U.S.A.'s hot air with metal gills.

Like a carried-over number in addition,
The sea comes up in the dark
And on the beach it leaves its delible mark,
And the unvarying, diastolic motion,
The repetitious, drugged sway of the ocean
Cradles a splinter adrift for a million years.
If you step sideways off the pier's
Edge, you'll continue to fall toward those tides
For a long, long time, your hands stiff at your sides,
But you will make no splash.

IV

The change of Empires is intimately tied
To the hum of words, the soft, fricative spray
Of spittle in the act of speech, the whole
Sum of Lobachevsky's angles, the strange way
That parallels may unwittingly collide
By casual chance some day
As longitudes contrive to meet at the pole.

And the change is linked as well to the chopping of wood,
To the tattered lining of life turned inside out
And thereby changed to a garment dry and good
(To tweed in winter, linen in a heat spell)
And the brain's kernel hardening in its shell.

In general, of all our organs the eye
Alone retains its elasticity,
Pliant, adaptive as a dream or wish.
For the change of Empires is linked with far-flung sight,
With the long gaze cast across the ocean's tide
(Somewhere within us lives a dormant fish)
And the mirror's revelation that the part in your hair
That you meticulously placed on the left side
Mysteriously shows up on the right,

Linked to weak gums, to heartburn brought about
By a diet unfamiliar and alien,
To the intense blankness, to the pristine white
Of the mind, which corresponds to the plain, small
Blank page of letterpaper on which you write.
But now the giddy pen
Points out resemblances, for after all,

The device in your hand is the same old pen and ink
As before, the woodland plants exhibit no change
Of leafage, and the same old bombers range
The clouds toward who knows what
Precisely chosen, carefully targeted spot.
And what you really need now is a drink.

V

New England towns seem much as if they were cast
Ashore along its coastline, beached by a flood-
Tide, and shining in darkness mile after mile

73

With imbricate, speckled scales of shingle and tile,
Like schools of sleeping fish hauled in by the vast
Nets of a continent that was first discovered
By herring and by cod. But neither cod

Nor herring have had any noble statues raised
In their honor, even though the memorial date
Could be comfortably omitted. As for the great
Flag of the place, it bears no blazon or mark
Of the first fish-founder among its parallel bars,
And as Louis Sullivan might perhaps have said,
Seen in the dark,
It looks like a sketch of towers thrust among stars.

Stifling. A man on his porch has wound a towel
Around his throat. A pitiful, small moth
Batters the window screen and bounces off
Like a bullet that Nature has zeroed in on itself
From an invisible ambush,
Aiming for some improbable bullseye
Right smack in the middle of July.

Because watches keep ticking, pain washes away
With the years. If time picks up the knack
Of panacea, it's because time can't abide
Being rushed, or finally turns insomniac.
And walking or swimming, the dreams of one hemisphere
        (heads)
Swarm with the nightmares, the dark, sinister play
Of its opposite (tails), its double, its underside.

Stifling. Great motionless plants. A distant bark.
A nodding head now jerks itself upright
To keep faces and phone numbers from sliding into the dark
And off the precarious edge of memory.
In genuine tragedy

It's not the fine hero that finally dies, it seems,
But, from constant wear and tear, night after night,
The old stage set itself, giving way at the seams.

VI

Since it's too late by now to say "goodbye"
And expect from time and space any reply
Except an echo that sounds like "here's your tip,"
Pseudo-majestic, cubing every chance
Word that escapes the lip,
I write in a sort of trance,

I write these words out blindly, the scrivening hand
Attempting to outstrip
By a second the "how come?"
That at any moment might escape the lip,
The same lip of the writer,
And sail away into night, there to expand
By geometrical progress, *und so weiter*.

I write from an Empire whose enormous flanks
Extend beneath the sea. Having sampled two
Oceans as well as continents, I feel that I know
What the globe itself must feel: there's nowhere to go.
Elsewhere is nothing more than a far-flung strew
Of stars, burning away.

Better to use a telescope to see
A snail self-sealed to the underside of a leaf.
I always used to regard "infinity"
As the art of splitting a liter into three
Equal components with a couple of friends
Without a drop left over. Not, through a lens,
An aggregate of miles without relief.

Night. A cuckoo wheezes in the Waldorf-
Inglorious. The legions close their ranks
And, leaning against cohorts, sleep upright.
Circuses pile against fora. High in the night
Above the bare blue-print of an empty court,
Like a lost tennis-ball, the moon regards its court,
A chess queen's dream, spare, parqueted, formal and bright.
There's no life without furniture.

VII

Only a corner cordoned off and laced
By dusty cobwebs may properly be called
Right-angled; only after the musketry of applause
And "bravos" does the actor rise from the dead;
Only when the fulcrum is solidly placed
Can a person lift, by Archimedian laws,
The weight of this world. And only that body whose weight
Is balanced at right angles to the floor
Can manage to walk about and navigate.

Stifling. There's a cockroach mob in the stadium
Of the zinc washbasin, crowding around the old
Corpse of a dried-up sponge. Turning its crown,
A bronze faucet, like Caesar's laureled head,
Deposes upon the living and the dead
A merciless column of water in which they drown.

The little bubble-beads inside my glass
Look like the holes in cheese.
No doubt that gravity holds sway,
Just as upon a solid mass,
Over such small transparencies as these.
And its accelerating waterfall
(Thirty-two feet per sec. per sec.) refracts
As does a ray of light in human clay.

Only the stacked, white china on the stove
Could look so much like a squashed, collapsed pagoda.
Space lends itself just to repeatable things,
Roses, for instance. If you see one alone,
You instantly see two. The bright corona,
The crimson petals abuzz, acrawl with wings
Of dragonflies, of wasps and bees with stings.

Stifling. Even the shadow on the wall,
Servile and weak as it is, still mimics the rise
Of the hand that wipes the forehead's sweat. The smell
Of old body is even clearer now
Than body's outline. Thought loses its defined
Edges, and the frazzled mind
Goes soft in its soup-bone skull. No one is here
To set the proper focus of your eyes.

VIII

Preserve these words against a time of cold,
A day of fear : Man survives like a fish,
Stranded, beached, but intent
On adapting itself to some deep, cellular wish,
Wriggling toward bushes, forming hinged leg-struts, then
To depart (leaving a track like the scrawl of a pen)
For the interior, the heart of the continent.

Full-breasted sphinxes there are, and lions winged
Like fanged and mythic birds.
Angels in white, as well, and nymphs of the sea.
To one who shoulders the vast obscurity
Of darkness and heavy heat (may one add, grief?)
They are more cherished than the concentric, ringed
Zeroes that ripple outwards from dropped words.

Even space itself, where there's nowhere to sit down,
Declines, like a star in its ether, its cold sky.
Yet just because shoes exist and the foot is shod
Some surface will always be there, some place to stand,
A portion of dry land.
And its brinks and beaches will be enchanted by
The soft song of the cod:

"Time is far greater than space. Space is a thing.
Whereas time is, in essence, the thought, the conscious dream
Of a thing. And life itself is a variety
Of time. The carp and bream
Are its clots and distillates. As are even more stark
And elemental things, including the sea-
Wave and the firmament of the dry land.
Including death, that punctuation mark.

At times, in that chaos, that piling up of days,
The sound of a single word rings in the ear,
Some brief, syllabic cry,
Like 'love,' perhaps, or possibly merely 'hi!'
But before I can make it out, static or haze
Trouble the scanning lines that undulate
And wave like the loosened ripples of your hair."

IX

Man broods over his life like night above a lamp.
At certain moments a thought takes leave of one
Of the brain's hemispheres, and slips, as a bedsheet might,
From under the restless sleeper's body-clamp,
Revealing who-knows-what-under-the-sun.
Unquestionably, night

Is a bulky thing, but not so infinite
As to engross both lobes. By slow degrees
The africa of the brain, its europe, the asian mass of it,
As well as other prominences in its crowded seas,
Creaking on their axis, turn a wrinkled cheek
Toward the electric heron with its lightbulb of a beak.

Behold: Aladdin says "Sesame!" and presto! there's a golden
     trove.
Caesar calls for his Brutus down the dark forum's colonnades.
In the jade pavilion a nightingale serenades
The Mandarin on the delicate theme of love.
A young girl rocks a cradle in the lamp's arena of light.
A naked Papuan leg keeps up a boogie-woogie beat.

Stifling. And so, cold knees tucked snug against the night,
It comes to you all at once, there in the bed,
That this is marriage. That beyond the customs sheds
Across dozens of borders there turns upon its side
A body you now share nothing with, unless
It be the ocean's bottom, hidden from sight,
And the experience of nakedness.

Nevertheless, you won't get up together.
Because, while it may be light way over there,
The dark still governs in your hemisphere.
One solar source has never been enough
To serve two average bodies, not since the time
God glued the world together in its prime.
The light has never been enough.

X

I notice a sleeve's hem, as my eyes fall,
And an elbow bending itself. Coordinates show
My location as paradise, that sovereign, blessed

Place where all purpose and longing is set at rest.
This is a planet without vistas, with no
Converging lines, with no prospects at all.

Touch the table-corner, touch the sharp nib of the pen
With your fingertip : you can tell such things could hurt.
And yet the paradise of the inert
Resides in pointedness;
Whereas in the lives of men
It is fleeting, a misty, mutable excess
That will not come again.

I find myself, as it were, on a mountain peak.
Beyond me there is . . . Chronos and thin air.
Preserve these words. The paradise men seek
Is a dead end, a worn-out, battered cape
Bent into crooked shape,
A cone, a finial cap, a steel ship's bow
From which the lookout never shouts "Land Ho!"

All you can tell for certain is the time.
That said, there's nothing left but to police
The revolving hands. The eye drowns silently
In the clock-face as in a broad, bottomless sea.
In paradise all clocks refuse to chime
For fear they might, in striking, disturb the peace.

Double all absences, multiply by two
Whatever's missing, and you'll have some clue
To what it's like here. A number, in any case,
Is also a word and, as such, a device
Or gesture that melts away without a trace,
Like a small cube of ice.

XI

Great issues leave a trail of words behind,
Free-form as clouds of tree-tops, rigid as dates
Of the year. So too, decked out in a paper hat,
The body viewing the ocean. It is selfless, flat
As a mirror as it stands in the darkness there.
Upon its face, just as within its mind,
Nothing but spreading ripples anywhere.

Consisting of love, of dirty words, a blend
Of ashes, the fear of death, the fragile case
Of the bone, and the groin's jeopardy, an erect
Body at sea-side is the foreskin of space,
Letting semen through. His cheek tear-silver-flecked,
Man juts forth into Time; man is his own end.

The Eastern end of the Empire dives into night—
Throat-high in darkness. The coil of the inner ear,
Like a snail's helix, faithfully repeats
Spirals of words in which it seems to hear
A voice of its own, and this tends to incite
The vocal chords, but it doesn't help you see.
In the realm of Time, no precipice creates
An echo's formal, answering symmetry.

Stifling. Only when lying flat on your back
Can you launch, with a sigh, your dry speech toward those
        mute,
Infinite regions above. With a soft sigh.
But the thought of the land's vastness, your own minute
Size in comparison, swings you forth and back
From wall to wall, like a cradle's rock-a-bye.

Therefore, sleep well. Sweet dreams. Knit up that sleeve.
Sleep as those only do who have gone pee-pee.
Countries get snared in maps, never shake free

Of their net of latitudes. Don't ask who's there
If you think the door is creaking. Never believe
The person who might reply and claim he's there.

XII

The door is creaking. A cod stands at the sill.
He asks for a drink, naturally, for God's sake.
You can't refuse a traveler a nip.
You indicate to him which road to take,
A winding highway, and wish him a good trip.
He takes his leave, but his identical

Twin has got a salesman's foot in the door.
(The two fish are as duplicate as glasses.)
All night a school of them come visiting.
But people who make their homes along the shore
Know how to sleep, have learned how to ignore
The measured tread of these approaching masses.

Sleep. The land beyond you is not round.
It is merely long, with various dip and mound,
Its ups and downs. Far longer is the sea.
At times, like a wrinkled forehead, it displays
A rolling wave. And longer still than these
Is the strand of matching beads of countless days;

And nights; and beyond these, the blindfold mist,
Angels in paradise, demons down in hell.
And longer a hundredfold than all of this
Are the thoughts of life, the solitary thought
Of death. And ten times that, longer than all,
The queer, vertiginous thought of Nothingness.

But the eye can't see that far. In fact, it must
Close down its lid to catch a glimpse of things.
Only this way—in sleep—can the eye adjust
To proper vision. Whatever may be in store,
For good or ill, in the dreams that such sleep brings
Depends on the sleeper. A cod stands at the door.

LAGOON

I

Down in the lobby three elderly women, bored,
Take up, with their knitting, the Passion of Our Lord
      As the universe and the tiny realm
Of the *pension "Accademia,"* side by side,
With TV blaring, sail into Christmastide,
      A look out desk-clerk at the helm.

II

And a nameless lodger, a nobody, boards the boat,
A bottle of grappa concealed in his raincoat
      As he gains his shadowy room, bereaved
Of memory, homeland, son, with only the noise
Of distant forests to grieve for his former joys,
      If anyone is grieved.

III

Venetian churchbells, tea cups, mantle clocks,
Chime and confound themselves in this stale box
      Of assorted lives. The brazen, coiled
Octopus-chandelier appears to be licking,
In a triptych mirror, bedsheet and mattress ticking,
      Sodden with tears and passion-soiled.

IV

Blown by nightwinds, an Adriatic tide
Floods the canals, boats rock from side to side,
      Moored cradles, and the humble bream,
Not ass and oxen, guards the rented bed
Where the windowblind above your sleeping head
      Moves to the sea-star's guiding beam.

V

So this is how we cope, putting out the heat
Of grappa with nightstand water, carving the meat
      Of flounder instead of Christmas roast,
So that Thy earliest back-boned ancestor
Might feed and nourish us, O Savior,
      This winter night on a damp coast.

VI

A Christmas without snow, tinsel or tree,
At the edge of a map-and-land corseted sea;
      Having scuttled and sunk its scallop shell,
Concealing its face while flaunting its backside,
Time rises from the goddess's frothy tide,
      Yet changes nothing but clock-hand and bell.

VII

A drowning city, where suddenly the dry
Light of reason dissolves in the moisture of the eye;
      Its winged lion, that can read and write,

Southern kin of northern Sphinxes of renown,
Won't drop his book and holler, but calmly drown
       In splinters of mirror, splashing light.

VIII

The gondola knocks against its moorings. Sound
Cancels itself, hearing and words are drowned,
       As is that nation where among
Forests of hands the tyrant of the State
Is voted in, its only candidate,
       And spit goes ice-cold on the tongue.

IX

So let us place the left paw, sheathing its claws,
In the crook of the arm of the other one, because
       This makes a hammer-and-sickle sign
With which to salute our era and bestow
A mute *Up Yours Even Unto The Elbow*
       Upon the nightmares of our time.

X

The raincoated figure is settling into place
Where Sophia, Constance, Prudence, Faith and Grace
       Lack futures, the only tense that is
Is present, where either a goyish or yiddish kiss
Tastes bitter, like the city, where footsteps fade
       Invisibly along the colonnade,

XI

Trackless and blank as a gondola's passage through
A water surface, smoothing out of view
  The measured wrinkles of its path,
Unmarked as a broad "So long!" like the wide piazza's space,
Or as a cramped "I love," like the narrow alleyways,
  Erased and without aftermath.

XII

Moldings and carvings, palaces and flights
Of stairs. Look up : the lion smiles from heights
  Of a tower wrapped as in a coat
Of wind, unbudged, determined not to yield,
Like a rank weed at the edge of a plowed field,
  And girdled round by Time's deep moat.

XIII

Night in St. Mark's piazza. A face as creased
As a finger from its fettering ring released,
  Biting a nail, is gazing high
Into that *nowhere* of pure thought, where sight
Is baffled by the bandages of night,
  Serene, beyond the naked eye,

Lagoon

XIV

Where, past all boundaries and all predicates,
Black, white or colorless, vague, volatile states,
　　　Something, some object, comes to mind.
Perhaps a body. In our dim days and few,
The speed of light equals a fleeting view,
　　　Even when blackout robs us blind.

NOTES

> *Let me be given nourishment at your hands*
> *Since it's for you I perform my little dance.*
> *For I am the street-walker, Magdalen,*
> *And come the dawn I'll be on my way again,*
> *The beauty queen, Miss France.*

PAGE 31   "REM": Rapid Eye Movement—a physiologi-
           cal indicator that a sleeper is dreaming.

PAGE 35   Horace, BK. I, ODE V

PAGE 45   "Of Byron writing, 'Many a fine day' ": "I
           should, many a good day, have blown my
           brains out, but for the recollection that it
           would have given pleasure to my mother-in-
           law . . ." From a letter to Tom Moore, Janu-
           ary 28, 1817.

PAGE 46   "Byron confessed to: 'If I should reach old
           age' ": "But I feel something, which makes me
           think that if I ever reach near to old age, like
           Swift, I shall die at 'top' first." From a diary
           of 1821. Once, pointing at a lightning-blasted
           oak, Swift had said to Edward Young, about
           his apprehensions of approaching madness, "I
           shall be like that tree. I shall die first at the
           top."

PAGE 47   "Young Henry Fuseli, . ." Johann Heinrich
           Füssli, later known as John Henry Fuseli, born
           in Zurich, February 6, 1741, died in London,
           April 16, 1825. Ordained a Zwinglian min-
           ister in 1761, but abandoned the ministry,
           first for literature and later for painting.
           Settled in London in 1779, where he was
           elected to the Royal Academy in 1790. He was
           a friend of Blake, and *The Nightmare* is prob-
           ably his best-known painting.

PAGE 51   "Miller of Dee":

                    There was a jolly miller once,
                        Lived on the river Dee;

> *He worked and sang from morn till night,*
> *No lark more blithe than he.*

> *And this the burden of his song*
> *Forever used to be—*
> *I care for nobody, no, not I,*
> *And nobody cares for me.*

PAGE 63   "As through those gutters of which Swift once wrote": "A Description of a City Shower," Oct. 1710.

PAGE 71   "I beheld new heavens, I beheld the earth made new" is an ironic echo of Isaiah 65:17—"For, behold, I create new heavens, and a new earth; and the former shall not be remembered, nor come into mind." The blessedness of being allowed to forget the old and ruined life is clearly connected in this poem with getting drunk.

PAGES 77 & 80   "Preserve these words," a phrase which occurs both in Section VIII and Section X, is an echo of a Mandelstam poem, addressed and dedicated to Anna Akhmatova, which, in the translation by Clarence Brown and W. S. Merwin, begins, "Keep my words forever for their aftertaste of misfortune and smoke."

PAGE 86   "northern Sphinxes": sculptured figures placed along the embankments of the Neva River in St. Petersburg.

ANTHONY HECHT

Anthony Hecht's first book of poems, A SUMMON-ING OF STONES, *appeared in 1954. He is also the author of* THE HARD HOURS, *which won the Pulitzer prize for poetry in 1968 and of* MILLIONS OF STRANGE SHADOWS, *1977. He is the translator (with Helen Bacon) of Aeschylus'* SEVEN AGAINST THEBES *in 1973, and co-editor (with John Hollander) in 1967 of a volume of light verse,* JIGGERY-POKERY. *He has taught at Kenyon, Bard, The State University of Iowa, and New York University. He has been a visiting professor at Harvard, and is presently the John H. Deane Professor of Poetry & Rhetoric at the University of Rochester.*